10 ↗ 8 🔱 Dr Neelon

P9-DOF-507

Ultra sound of carotid artery CT scan (HEART)
a good indicator of susceptibility to
stroke

Cholesteral (most) made in the
liver STATINS block enzymes that help
make cholesteral

Phase I 50/100 II 200 III 700 mg SODIUM
4000 mg — Avg Am day's intake

Diabetic retinopathy cured by low
sodium diet.

Cannot live on 0 g sodium
Blow up like a balloon — mechanism
is cranked up to save it all.

SALARY → comes from the word salt
"not worth his salt"

SILVER
DEPARTURES

A Collection of Quotations
Compiled by
Richard Kehl

A Star & Elephant Book

1983

Text copyright © 1983 by Richard Kehl
Cover pictures copyright © 1983 by Richard Kehl
First Edition • Second Printing
A Star & Elephant Book
The Green Tiger Press
La Jolla, California
92038

Paperbound ISBN 0-88138-014-8

These quotations were gathered over many years of reading. When I copied them down it was with no thought of publication. I kept them because of their power over me. As a consequence they are imperfectly attributed, and may be incorrectly worded in a few instances. To their authors, living and dead, my thanks, and where appropriate, my apologies.

Richard Kehl

Set out from any point. They are all alike. They all lead to a point of departure.

Antonio Porchia

The only real progress lies in learning to be wrong all alone.

Albert Camus

Angels fly because they take themselves lightly.

Jean Cocteau

I think that if I recall something, for example, if today I look back on this morning, then I get an image of what I saw this morning. But if tonight, I'm thinking back on this morning, then what I'm really recalling is not the first image, but the first image in memory. So that every time I recall something, I'm not recalling it really, I'm recalling the last time I recalled it. I'm recalling my last memory of it. So that really, I have no memories whatever. I have no images whatever, about my childhood, about my youth.

Jorge Luis Borges

We are asleep with compasses in our hands.

W.S. Merwin

Silver Departures

There are just some things no one can do alone: conspire, be a mob, or a choir, or a regiment. Or elope.

Renata Adler

No snowflake ever falls in the wrong place.

Zen

Perhaps all the dragons of our lives are princesses who are only waiting to see us once beautiful and brave.

Rainer Maria Rilke

The first step . . . shall be to lose the way.

Galway Kinnell

If you want to see how you look asleep, stand in front of a mirror with your eyes shut.

Author Unknown

When I sit down to make a sketch from nature, the first thing I try to do is, to forget that I have ever seen a picture.

John Constable

The difference between the right word and the almost right word is the difference between lightning and the lightning bug.

Mark Twain

We all know the man whom children or dogs love instinctively. It is a rare gift to be able to inspire this affection. The fates have been kind to him. But to inspire the affection of inanimate things is something greater. The man to whom a collar or a window sash takes instinctively is a man who may truly be said to have luck on his side.

A.A. Milne

"A pier," Stephen said, "Yes, a disappointed bridge."

James Joyce

One must ask children and birds how cherries and strawberries taste.

Johann Wolfgang Goethe

When Gandhi was asked what he thought of western civilization, he said, "It would be nice."

Silver Departures

"Stay," he said, his right arm around her waist and her face expectantly turned to him, "shall it be the kiss pathetic, sympathetic, graphic, paragraphic, Oriental, intellectual, paroxysmal quick and dismal, slow and unctuous, long and tedious, devotional, or what?" She said perhaps that would be the better way.

Charles Bousbaugh

I have woven a parachute out of everything broken.

William Stafford

After an hour or so in the woods looking for mushrooms, Dad said, "Well, we can always go and buy some real ones."

John Cage

The future is but the obsolete in reverse.

Vladimir Nabokov

There's an alternative. There's always a third way, and it's not a combination of the other two ways. It's a different way.

David Carradine

The British during World War II came up with some imaginative ideas. One was to freeze the clouds, move them along the coast of Southern England, and use them as platforms for anti-aircraft guns.

Beautiful, like the chance meeting of a sewing machine and an umbrella on a dissecting table.

Comte de Lautréamont

"Therefore" is a word the poet must not know.

André Gide

In a letter to Henri Moudor who had sent her a black lead drawing of a rose, Colette wrote: "I am looking at it through my magnifying glass, and thank God, I can discover nothing; you have left it all its mystery."

Sit, walk, or run, but don't wobble.

Zen

My happiest experience in reading plays occurred during the Group Theatre days. A script had been submitted which began; "Act One: Ten thousand years before the creation of man. Act Two: Two weeks later."

Harold Clurman

Silver Departures

And if you still find something, you have not lost
everything. You still have to lose something.

Antonio Porchia

We must work at the future as weavers work at
highwarp tapestry: without seeing it.

Anatole France

To be a poet of life, though artists seldom
realize it, is the *summum*. To breathe out more
than one breathes in.

Henry Miller

Among these unfinished tales is that of Mr.
James Phillimore, who, stepping back into his
house to get his umbrella, was never more seen in
this world.

Arthur Conan Doyle

The problem is not whether the song will
continue, but whether a dark space can be found
where the notes can resonate.

Rainer Maria Rilke

Language is fossil poetry.

Ralph Waldo Emerson

Only the birds are able to throw off their shadow. The shadow always stays behind on earth. Our imagination flies. We are its shadow on the earth.

Vladimir Nabokov

The poet doesn't invent. He listens.

Jean Cocteau

Never mind. The self is the least of it. Let our scars fall in love.

Galway Kinnell

He liked to go from A to B without inventing letters between.

John McPhee

When a dog runs at you, whistle for him.

Henry David Thoreau

Things that I longed for in vain and things that I got — let them pass. Let me but truly possess the things that I ever spurned and overlooked.

Author Unknown

Silver Departures

"Doesn't it bore you," I asked her one day when we were out walking, "to return by the same way?" "It's not the same way because we're going backwards."

Maurice Goudeket to Colette.

Include the knower in the known.

Julian Jaynes

Actually, I'm not all that interested in the subject of photography. Once the picture is in the box, I'm not all that interested in what happens next. Hunters, after all, usually aren't cooks.

Henri Cartier-Bresson

It is the material of all things loose and set afloat that makes my sea.

Herman Melville

The atoms and molecules within you dream they are people.

from the Seth Tapes

Whether it happened so or not I do not know; but if you think about it you can see that it is true.

Black Elk

I imitate everyone except myself.

Pablo Picasso

"I have also thought of a model city from which I deduce all the others," Marco answered. "It is a city made only of exceptions, exclusions, incongruities, contradictions. If such a city is the most improbable, by reducing the number of abnormal elements, we increase the probability that the city really exists. So I have only to subtract exceptions from my model, and in whatever direction I proceed, I will arrive at one of the cities which, always as an exception, exist. But I cannot force my operation beyond a certain limit: I would achieve cities too probable to be real."

Italo Calvino

We have given the distances birthdays.

Robert Dana

Balzac's dread of being photographed was that . . . everybody in their natural state was made up of a series of ghostly images superimposed in layers to infinity, wrapped in infinitesimal films . . . each Daguerrian operation was therefore going to lay hold of, detach, and use up one of the layers of the body on which it focused.

Her hearing was keener than his, and she heard silences he was unaware of.

D.M. Thomas

I will take with me the emptiness of my hands. What you do not have you find everywhere.

W.S. Merwin

The Working Brain: We often think that when we have completed our study of *one* we know all about *two,* because "two" is "one and one." We forget that we still have to make a study of "and."

A. Eddington

Stay a while longer. The butterflies will die and one of us will say, "Look, it is tomorrow already" . . . and one of us will say, "Yes, it is still tomorrow."

Author Unknown

We are what we pretend to be, so we must be careful about what we pretend to be.

Kurt Vonnegut, Jr.

Make your ego porous. Will is of little impor- tance, complaining is nothing, fame is nothing. Openness, patience, receptivity, solitude is everything.

Rainer Maria Rilke

This has been a most wonderful evening. Gertrude has said things tonight it'll take her ten years to understand.

Alice B. Toklas

Crops like mine are not so much planted as buried.

Peter Davison

I begin with what was always gone.

W.S. Merwin

The poet's heart, like all other hearts, is an interminable artichoke.

Pablo Neruda

The Zen monk Bassui wrote a letter to one of his disciples who was about to die, and in it he said: "Your end which is endless is as a snowflake dissolving in the pure air." The snowflake, which was once very much a discernible subsystem of the universe, now dissolves into the larger system which once held it. Though it is no longer present as a distinct subsystem, its essence is somehow present, and will remain so. It floats in Tumbolia, along with hiccups that are not being hiccuped and characters in stories that are not being read.

Douglas Hofstader

Mr. S.B., blind from the age of ten months, his sight returned when he was over fifty: S.B. was astonished to see a crescent moon, and asked what it was. He had always imagined the quarter moon would look like a quarter piece of cake.

The next message you need is always right where you are.

Ram Dass

Be happy. It's one way of being wise.

Colette

"Not out but through!"

Aniela Jaffe

A throw of the dice will never abolish chance.

Marcel Duchamp

What is most admirable in the fantastic is that the fantastic doesn't exist; all is real.

André Breton

The last Japanese character written in this life by Soen Roshi's venerable teacher, and the last word spoken, was the word for "dream."

Each language performs an artificial chopping up of the continuous flow of existence in a different way. Children repattern every day. Mississippi is not Mrs. Sippy, the equator is not a menagerie lion but an imaginary line.

Adam Smith

Silence moves faster when it's going backward.

Jean Cocteau

Only the dreamer can change the dream.

John Logan

We are what we imagine. Our very existence consists in our imagination of ourselves. The greatest tragedy that can befall us is to go unimagined.

N. Scott Momaday

I knew of a physicist at the University of Chicago who was rather crazy like some scientists, and the idea of the insolidity, the instability of the physical world, impressed him so much that he used to go around in enormous padded slippers for fear he should fall through the floor.

Alan Watts

Silver Departures

Blind people don't have the faintest idea what darkness is.

Author Unknown

The stars sew with too fine a thread.

Eugenio Montale

Heart, I told you before and twice, and three times, don't knock at that door. No one will answer.

Anonymous Spanish folk song

The little I know, I owe to my ignorance.

Sacha Guitry

It is as if I were attempting to trace with the point of a pencil the shadow of the tracing pencil.

Nathanael West

The thing that astonished him was that cats should have two holes cut in their coat exactly at the place where their eyes are.

George C. Lichtenberg

Freedom of will is the ability to do gladly that which I must do.

Carl Jung

Deafness isn't the opposite of hearing, it's a silence full of sounds.

Mark Medoff

James Thurber once sat by his window watching men cut down elm trees to clear a site for an institution in which to confine people who had been driven insane by the cutting down of elm trees.

I am a lie that always tells the truth.

Jean Cocteau

There is nothing I can do for you and I am doing it, and that is poetry.

Frank O'Hara

When you're learning, you're burning — putting out a lot of heat. When you're all burned up, then you become light.

Da Free John

We say "seeing is believing," but actually, as Santayana pointed out, we are all much better at believing than at seeing. In fact, we are seeing what we believe nearly all the time and only occasionally seeing what we can't believe.

Robert Anton Wilson

Specialization is for insects.

Robert Heinlein

I really think I write about everyday life. I don't think I'm quite as odd as others say I am. Life is intrinsically, well, boring and dangerous at the same time. At any given moment the floor may open up. Of course, it almost never does; that's what makes it so boring.

Edward Gorey

Quite literally, a man's memory is what he forgets with.

Author Unknown

The immature poet imitates; the mature poet plagiarizes.

T.S. Eliot

Fame is a comic distinction shared with Roy Rogers' horse and Miss Watermelon of 1955.

Flannery O'Connor

One does not dream; one is dreamed. We undergo the dream, we are the objects.

Carl Jung

If the angel deigns to come, it will be because you have convinced him, not by tears, but by your humble resolve to be always beginning: to be a beginner.

Rainer Maria Rilke

Whatever I take, I take too much or too little; I do not take the exact amount. The exact amount is no use to me.

Antonio Porchia

"The horror of that moment," exclaimed the King, in *Alice Through The Looking-Glass,* "I shall never, never forget!" "You will, though," the Queen said, "If you don't make a memorandum of it."

Lewis Carroll

I was always an avid forgetter: in my two human hands only the untouchable things of the world live unscathed.

Pablo Neruda

The silver question — is the one you are always afraid to ask. (and the answer is yes).

Debora Greger

Sharp nostalgia, infinite and terrible, for what I already possess.

Juan Ramón Jimenez

We begin life with the world presenting itself to us as it is. Someone — our parents, teachers, analysts — hypnotizes us to "see" the world and construe it in the "right" way. These others label the world, attach names and give voices to the beings and events in it, so that thereafter, we cannot read the world in any other language or hear it saying other things to us. The task is to break the hypnotic spell, so that we become undeaf, unblind and multilingual, thereby letting the world speak to us in new voices and write all its possible meanings in the new book of our existence. Be careful in your choice of hypnotists.

Sidney Jourard

Earth, isn't this what you want — invisibly to arise in us? Is it not your dream to be some day invisible?

Rainer Maria Rilke

They always told me when I was young, "Just wait, and you'll see." Now I'm old and see nothing. It's wonderful.

Eric Satie

It took me a long time to discover that the key
thing in acting is honesty. Once you know how to
fake that, you've got it made.

Actor in *Peyton Place*

And that heart which was a wild garden was
given to him who loved only trim lawns. And the
imbecile carried the princess into slavery.

Antoine de St. Exupery

Have all the keys removed from your typewriter
except the ones needed to spell her name.

Author Unknown

The highest form of operational thinking: the
ability to hypothetically consider any state along
a continuum of possibility as potentially equal to
any other state, and return to the same state from
which the operation began.

Jean Piaget

Tying his tie and whistling a tune Zimmer
strikes a nostalgic note and invents his past.

Annie Dillard

When anyone reads this but you it begins to be
lost.

Author Unknown

Silver Departures

On a hot day in the southern desert of Africa
I had wanted to go and speak to one of my
favourite Stone Age hunters. He was sitting in the
middle of a thorn bush. . . . He was huddled in an
attitude of the most intense concentration . . . but
his friends would not let me get near him, saying,
"But don't you know, he is doing work of the
utmost importance. He is making clouds."

Laurens Van der Post

One must bear in mind one thing. It isn't
necessary to know what that thing is.

John Ashbery

Then you could be eligible for such an ineffable
compliment as the one that a lady paid to the
sculpture of David Tolerton: "Is it real," she asked,
"or did you make it?"

We learn nothing from the things we know.

John Cage

My final belief is suffering. And I begin to believe
that I do not suffer.

Antonio Porchia

If you want to know the taste of a pear, you must change the pear by eating it yourself.

Mao Tse Tung

For me the only realist is the visionary because he bears witness to his own reality.

Federico Fellini

The most beautiful thing we can experience is the mysterious. It is the source of all true art and science. He to whom the emotion is a stranger, who can no longer pause and stand wrapped in awe, is as good as dead; his eyes are closed.

Albert Einstein

The way to learn any game is to play for more than you can afford to lose.

Author Unknown

What can a flame remember? If it remembers a little less than is necessary, it goes out; if it remembers a little more than is necessary, it goes out. If only it could teach us, while it burns, to remember correctly.

George Seferis

I am trying to be unfamiliar with what I'm doing.

John Cage

*Silver
Departures*

Today is obsolete.

Walter Lowenfels

The fifteen-year old daughter of a friend
once addressed the old Jung as follows: "Herr
Professor, you are so clever. Could you please tell
me the shortest path to my life's goal?" Without a
moment's hesitation Jung replied, "The detour!"

The word "water" is itself undrinkable, and the
formula H_2O will not float a ship.

Alan Watts

Who has not sat before his own heart's curtain?
It lifts: and the scenery is falling apart.

Rainer Maria Rilke

It all began with my "eye-trapper" when I was a
little boy. I used to close my eyes and turn around
three times. I believed that way I could trap the air,
the scents, the life that surrounded me. The trap
didn't work very well, but I never got over the idea
of it.

Jacques Henri Lartigue

If you think you're free, there's no escape
possible.

Ram Dass

A photograph is a secret about a secret. The more it tells you the less you know.

Diane Arbus

You do not need to leave your room. Remain sitting at your table and listen. Do not even listen, simply wait. Do not even wait, be quite still and solitary. The world will freely offer itself to you to be unmasked, it has no choice, it will roll in ecstasy at your feet.

Franz Kafka

To see is to forget the name of the thing one sees.

Paul Valéry

While I work I leave my body outside the door, the way Moslems take off their shoes before entering the mosque.

Pablo Picasso

The poet is one who is able to keep the fresh vision of the child alive within the mature man.

Anaïs Nin

There is no avant garde. There are only people who are a little late.

Edgar Varese

Every decision you make is a mistake.

Edward Dahlberg

In the palm of one hand now the rain falls. From the other the grass grows. What can I tell you?

Vasko Popa

Sanity is the most profound moral option of our time.

Renata Adler

There is the wire Chesterton sent to his wife while away from home to deliver a lecture in a town in the Midlands: "Am in Market Harborough. Where ought I to be?"

The heart is an infinity of massive chains, chaining little handfuls of air.

Antonio Porchia

The Chinese say that when you have too much trouble, you write poetry. There are two kinds of poetry: in one you jump in, in the other you jump out. If you jump out you become a philosopher. If you jump in you die with the poem.

Can you remember what remembering was like last Tuesday?

Ludwig Wittgenstein

"If no man is an island," cried Morris Irving Hyman, "I'm the narrowest peninsula in the world."

Veronica Porche

He was a great, you might say a dangerous, listener.

Karl Shapiro, of Randall Jarrell

Pasternak says life creates incidents to divert our attention from it so that it can get on with the work it can only accomplish unobserved.

You have to wake up a virgin each morning.

Jean-Louis Barrault

And somebody would come and knock on this air long after I have gone and there in front of me a life would open.

W.S. Merwin

Silver Departures

I know well enough that this image fixed forever
in my mind is not you, but the shadow of love
which exists in me . . . and although I know this,
I then think that without you, without the rare
excuse you gave me, my love, now a tenderness
today would be there within, sleeping still, and
lying in hope . . . then I thank you.

Luis Cernuda

The eagerness of objects to be what we are
afraid to do cannot help but move us.

Frank O'Hara

Everything one invents is true, you may be
perfectly sure of that. Poetry is as precise as
geometry.

Gustave Flaubert

Every toy has the right to break.

Antonio Porchia

Wanted: a needle swift enough to sew this
poem into a blanket.

Charles Simic

Dissillusion is the last illusion.

Wallace Stevens

"Daddy, are we live or on tape?"

The final poem will be the poem of fact in the
language of fact, but it will be the poem of fact not
realized before.

Wallace Stevens

Close one sad eye. Yes. Close the other sad eye.
Yes. I can see now.

Yehuda Amichai

. . . a man of knowledge lives by acting, not by
thinking about acting, nor by thinking about what
he will think when he has finished acting. A man
of knowledge chooses a path with heart and
follows it; and then he looks and rejoices and
laughs; and then he *sees* and knows.

Don Juan Matues

We do what only lovers can . . . make a gift out
of necessity.

Leonard Cohen

Carrying a medicine for which no one has
found the disease and hoping I would make it in
time.

Richard Shelton

My advice when watching movies is not to blink.

Sister Mary Corita

In a field, I am the absence of field. This is always the case. Wherever I am, I am what is missing.

Mark Strand

It takes a very long time to become young.

Pablo Picasso

Kids: they dance before they learn there is anything that isn't music.

William Stafford

I once knew a crazy woman who worked her hands in the air . . . she made sculptures in the air. I didn't think she was doing anything. But, since she was crazy, she used flour for makeup. She was always making immobile sculptures in the air. But one day she moved her face and the flour fell from her face like a cloud covering up something in the air. And I saw a beautiful geometrical form. Then I took a bag of flour, went into her room and started to throw the flour around in the air. And beautiful sculptures began to appear. That's the story.

Alexandro Jodorowsky

My name is Might-have-been; I am also called
No-more, Too-late, Farewell.

Dante Gabriel Rossetti

Women and children first, then tap dancers.

Richard Kehl

Nothing is ever the same as they said it was. It's
what I've never seen before that I recognize.

Diane Arbus

Unjust. How many times I've used that word,
scolded myself with it. All I mean by it now is that I
don't have the final courage to say that I refuse to
preside over violations against myself, and to hell
with justice.

Lillian Hellman

Just remember, we're all in this alone.

Lily Tomlin

Perhaps to our senses things offer only their
rejections. Perfume is what the flowers throw
away.

Paul Valéry

Silver Departures

Ferraus cured a fever with the aid of a slip
of paper on which was written the two words
"Against Fever" from which the patient was to tear
off one letter each day and eat it.

Ostrander-Schroeder

Beware, as they say, of mistaking the finger for
the moon when you're pointing at it.

John Cage

I was right not to be afraid of any thief but
myself, who will end by leaving me nothing.

Katherine Anne Porter

Each moment is a place you've never been.

Mark Strand

The air pushes around you, fills with birds,
yellow wings and eyes.

Stephen Dobyns

Close your hand — do you feel an absence or a
presence?

Brenda Hefty

A child has much to learn before it can pretend.

Author Unknown

Man with wooden leg escapes prison. He's caught. They take his wooden leg away from him. Each day he must cross a large hill and swim a wide river to get to the field where he must work all day on one leg. This goes on for a year. At the Christmas Party they give him back his leg. Now he doesn't want it. His escape is all planned. It requires only one leg.

James Tate

What we remember can be changed. What we forget we are always.

Richard Shelton

The sort of man who, throwing a stone upon a ground, would miss.

Idries Shah

A little unlearning goes a long way.

Richard Kehl

Message to deep-sea diver: "Surface at once. Ship is sinking."

The best thing we can do is make wherever we're lost look as much like home as we can.

Roger Fry

Hold the map close to your face. Breathe into it,
and you will hear a river start. Open the map.

Greg Kuzma

It's a question too complicated to answer if you
put me up against a wall. And too simple to ask.

Penelope Gilliatt

Windows listen for announcements of broken
glass.

Author Unknown

The things of mine that are utterly lost are the
ones that, when I lost them, were not found by
someone else.

Antonio Porchia

A person can look at pointing in reverse, that is,
from finger tip to wrist.

Ludwig Wittgenstein

Artists have at least a form within which they
can hold their own conflicting opposites together.
But there are some who have no recognized
artistic form to serve this purpose. They are artists
of living. To my mind, these last are the supreme
heroes in our soulless society.

Irene Claremont de Castillejo

The point is, if there were only one person in the world, it would be impossible for that person to be insane.

Robert Pirsig

Lend yourself to others, but give yourself to yourself.

Michel de Montaigne

A printer brooding on the loss of the woman he loved, set her name in type and swallowed it.

Author Unknown

He was trying to frame a question that would take in all the questions and elicit an answer that would be all the answers, but it kept coming out so simple that he distrusted it.

Tom Stoppard

I ask about the sky, but the answer is about a rope.

Author Unknown

The trouble with men is men, the trouble with women, men.

Author Unknown

Silver Departures

Q. Do you believe that photography can be labeled art? A. That is ridiculous and vain. Everything is art. A cook, a shoemaker, a hairdresser are all artists according to how talented they are. This whole mess of labels and titles has nothing to do with me. I am absolutely indifferent to the noise and commotion. It isn't the medium that's important but the person that expresses himself through it. I just continue to look for those special moments, the way a fisherman does when he tells you, "They're biting today."

Jacques Henri Lartigue

I could have been a marvelous madman. I could have contained my madness.

Henri Langlois

Absence of evidence is not evidence of absence.

Author Unknown

Between yea and nay, how much difference is there?

Lao Tzu

There are a number of very important
irreversibles to be discovered in our universe.
One of them is that every time you make an
experiment you learn more: quite literally, *you
can not learn less.*

Buckminster Fuller

Mirrors would do well to think before they cast
their reflections back at us.

Jean Cocteau

We are led one thing at a time through gain to
that pure gain — all that we lose.

William Stafford

I work from awkwardness. By that I mean I
don't like to arrange things. If I stand in front of
something, instead of arranging it, I arrange
myself.

Diane Arbus

Dropped objects fall ever so slightly more
slowly than they used to, and each year the
average person's weight decreases — by about
one-millionth the weight of a potato chip.

Newspaper

Silver Departures

Personally I'm always ready to learn, although I do not always like being taught.

Winston Churchill

I think of that friend too much moved by music who turned to games and made a game of boredom, of that one too much loved by faces who turned his face to the wall, and of that marvelous liar who turned at last to truth.

Henri Coulette

An ideal map would contain the map of the map, the map of the map of the map . . . endlessly.

Alfred Korzybski

There is no reason why a kaleidoscope should not have as much fun as a telescope.

Mark Twain

In order for a proposition to be capable of being true, it must also be capable of being false.

Ludwig Wittgenstein

The whole work of a man really seems to consist in nothing but proving to himself every minute that he is a man and not a piano key.

Fyodor Dostoyevsky

You fall in love by suddenly knowing what past love hadn't.

John Fowles

I looked down and traced my foot in the dust and thought again and said, "OK — any star."

William Stafford

Everything we come across is to the point.

John Cage

Grownups never understand anything by themselves and it is tiresome for children to be always and forever explaining things to them.

Antoine de St. Exupéry

Not to dream boldly may turn out to be simply irresponsible.

George Leonard

What would there be in a story of happiness? Only what prepares it, only what destroys it can be told.

André Gide

And me, I am writing a poem for you. Look!
No hands.

Ruth Krauss

I'll figure out as best I can what I ought to do
and then do it. If I don't make any mistakes who
will believe my errors? I'll change my whole
person and then when I'm different and no one
can recognize me I'll keep doing the same things
that I did since I couldn't possibly do otherwise.

Pablo Neruda

And upsidedown in the earth a dead man walks
upon my soles when I walk.

Author Unknown

The poet does not keep what he discovers;
having transcribed it, soon loses it. Therein lies his
novelty, his infinity, and his peril.

René Char

I am going to school myself so well with things
that, when I try to explain my problems, I shall
speak, not of self, but of geography.

Pablo Neruda

Then you should say what you mean, the March Hare went on. "I do," Alice hastily replied. "At least — at least I mean what I say — that's the same thing you know." "Not the same thing a bit!" said the Hatter. "Why, you might just as well say that 'I see what I eat.' is the same thing as 'I eat what I see.' "

Lewis Carroll

The day was counting up its birds and never got the answer right.

Author Unknown

The science of imaginary solutions that examines the laws governing exceptions.

Author Unknown

In relief, in humiliation, in terror, he understood that he, too, was an appearance — that someone else was dreaming him.

Jorge Luis Borges

Dear Dr. Thosteson: My concern is that when I am in a dark room and start to cough, sparks fly from my mouth.

Newspaper

Silver Departures

Fear forgetting forgets remembering.

Author Unknown

If you take any activity, any art, any discipline, any skill, take it and push it as far as it will go, push it beyond where it has ever been before, push it to the wildest edge of edges, then you force it into the realm of magic.

Tom Robbins

The night is trying to teach the day how to pretend.

Richard Kehl

As soon as you have made a thought, laugh at it.

Lao Tzu

In the original score of Mozart's Horn Concerto #4 (K. 495), the writing breaks into inks in four colors playfully distributed through the music for visual effect only.

Responsibility is to keep the ability to respond.

Gustav Mahler

Between no place of mine and no place of yours, you'd have thought I'd know the way by now.

W.S. Merwin

Tomorrow I was going to the spring meadows to pick young greens. It snowed all day yesterday and snowed all day today.

Unknown Japanese Author

Every something is an echo of nothing.

Author Unknown

The situation reached the height of the ludicrous when I suddenly realized one day that of everything I had written about the man I could just as well have said the opposite. I had indubitably reached that dead end which lies so artfully hidden in the phrase "the meaning of meaning."

Henry Miller

How beautiful your cry that gives me your silence.

René Char

In the Highlands of New Guinea I saw men with photographs of themselves mounted on their foreheads, so they would be recognized.

Ted Carpenter

As though naturally erasers would speak the language of pencils.

Howard Nemerov

Today I was petting my dog and the 5 year-old next door said to me "I can see a planet in you. And everybody on it is petting puppy."

Anne Raymo

What we need is more people who specialize in the impossible.

Theodore Roethke

Solitude, my mother, tell me my life again.

O.V. de L. Milosz

He steps into the mirror, refusing to be anyone else.

Frank O'Hara

Our words misunderstand us.

Adrienne Rich

I never dreamed of being Shakespeare or Goethe, and I never expected to hold the great mirror of truth up before the world; I dreamed only of being a little pocket mirror, the sort that a woman can carry in her purse; one that reflects small blemishes, and some great beauties, when held close enough to the heart.

Peter Altenberg

Nothing in the universe can travel at the speed of light, they say, forgetful of the shadow's speed.

Howard Nemerov

Nothing is more imprecise than precision.

Eugene Ionesco

He brought so little to what he saw, he saw what was there.

Wright Morris

Now that the moon is out of a job, it has an easy climb.

William Stafford

Needn't be anything elaborate, he said. Echoes will be fine.

Richard Kehl

Where did the truth go? The key was mislaid in an army of doors, it was there on its ring with the others, but the lock is nowhere in the world. No world for the key to get lost in, no true or false, in the end.

Pablo Neruda

Picasso told me that he had seen in Avignon, on the square of the Chateau des Papes, an old painter, half-blind, who was painting the castle. His wife, standing beside him, looked at the castle through binoculars and described it to him. He was painting from his wife.

Jean Cocteau

By being both here and beyond I am becoming a horizon.

Mark Strand

We don't learn the word "dream" by being shown a dream, the way we learn the word "apple" by being shown an apple.

Author Unknown

Didn't Delacroix say that one of the finest "paintings" he had ever seen was a particularly handsome Persian rug he once came across?

The point is to be invisible or blinding, nothing in between.

Author Unknown

If I could only remember that the days were, not bricks to be laid row on row, to be built into a solid house, where one might dwell in safety and peace, but only food for the fires of the heart.

Edmund Wilson

Quit this world. Quit the next world. Quit quitting.

Ram Dass

Thoreau said that sounds are bubbles on the surface of silence.

Suppose someone claimed to have a microscopically exact replica (in marble, even) of Michelangelo's David in his home. When you go to see this marvel, you find a twenty-foot-tall roughly rectilinear hunk of pure white marble standing in his living room. "I haven't gotten around to *unpacking* it yet," he says, "but I know it's in there."

Douglas Hofstadter

Poetry is just the evidence of life. If your life is burning well, poetry is just the ash.

Leonard Cohen

Inside my empty bottle I was constructing a lighthouse while all the others were making ships.

Charles Simic

I am hoarse from silence.

Theodore Roethke

You know that, according to quantum theory, if two particles collide with enough energy you can, in principle, with an infinitesimal probability, produce two grand pianos.

I.I. Rabi

I used to be a design but now I'm a tree.

Eight-year old.

A man's work is nothing but this slow trek to rediscover, through the detours of art, those two or three great and simple images in whose presence his heart first opened.

Albert Camus

We are perceivers. We are an awareness. We are not objects. We are boundless. The world of objects and solidity is a way of making our passage on earth convenient. It is only a description that was created to help us.

Don Juan Mateus

I love you as you are, but do not tell me how that is.

Antonio Porchia

Ts' iu' Pen did not think of time as absolute and uniform. He believed in an infinite series of times, in a dizzily growing, ever spreading network of diverging, converging and parallel times. This web of time — the strands of which approach one another, bifurcate, intersect, or ignore each other through the centuries — embraces every possibility. We do not exist in most of them. In some you exist and not I, while in others I do and you do not, and in yet others both of us exist. In this one, in which chance has favored me, you have come to my gate. In another, you, crossing the garden, have found me dead. In yet another, I say these very same words, but am an error, a phantom.

Jorge Luis Borges

Silver Departures

What does the swallow know of the owl's insomnia?

Rafael Alberti

We keep our distance. It is all we have.

Richard Shelton

If I find a film dull, I find it infinitely more entertaining to watch the scratches.

Norman McLaren

Jean-Pierre Aumont says to André Gide, "May I ask you an indiscreet question?" To which Gide replies, "There are no indiscreet questions, there are only indiscreet answers."

I can't hear myself hearing.

Marcel Duchamp

If you don't get lost, there's a chance you may never be found.

Author Unknown

Using chalk to mark the rooms, so you will know if you've been there before.

Author Unknown

Reminds me of a passage in one of Schumann's piano sonatas marked, "As fast as possible," which is followed a few bars later with the admonition, "Faster."

Everything is relevant. I call it loving.

James Tate

The trouble with you, Robert, is that you make the visible world too easy to see.

Attributed to Wallace Stevens, after Robert Frost had allegedly complained about the obscurity of Stevens' poems

A certain selection and discretion must be used in producing a realistic effect.

Arthur Conan Doyle

That which we die for lives as wholly as that which we live for dies.

e.e. cummings

The greatest enemy of any one of our truths may be the rest of our truths.

William James

Silver Departures

The poem is the point at which our strength gave out.

Richard Rosen

We are not committed to this or that. We are committed to the nothing-in-between . . . whether we know it or not.

John Cage

Tu Fu served in the office of "Reminder" at the emperor's court.

How goes a life? Something like the ocean building dead coral.

Stanley Moss

I thought finally that of all the nostalgias that haunt the human heart the greatest of them all, for me, is an everlasting longing to bring what is youngest home to what is oldest, in us all.

Laurens Van der Post

When asked what he was, Duchamp said he was a "respirateur," a breather.

If I wanted to be consistent, I would have stayed home.

Author Unknown

I saved a snowflake for each single hour you were away.

Rainer Brambach

A 20th Century-Fox executive in Paris arranged for an exhibit of the fake paintings used in the movie *How To Steal A Million.* He phoned Howard Newman of the New York office, who said the fakes could not be shipped because they were on tour. "What should I do?" asked the Paris man frantically. "Get some originals," said Newman. "Nobody'll know the difference."

Be open, be available, be exposed, be skinless. Skinless? Dance around in your bones.

Wallace Stegner

To be abreast of the incurable.

Author Unknown

Man's mind is a mirror of a universe that mirrors man's mind.

Joseph Pearce

No trace: When you do something, you should
burn yourself completely, like a good bonfire,
leaving no trace of yourself.

Shunryu Suzuki

Remember, never sign a name you want
to keep.

Debora Greger

Death is patiently making my mask as I sleep.
Each morning I awake to discover in the corners
of my eyes the small tears of his wax.

Philip Dow

The years come to my door and knock and
walk away sighing.

Richard Tillinghast

Some years ago a young scholar who greatly
admired A.E. Housman's work wrote to the poet
and asked him how he managed always to select
the right word. Housman replied that he didn't
bother about trying to get the right word, he
simply bothered about getting rid of the wrong
one.

There is a blind butterfly in your ear.

James Tate

Since we are destined to live out our lives in the prison of our minds, our one duty is to furnish it well.

Peter Ustinov

Dreams are real while they last; can we say more of life?

Havelock Ellis

Suppose someone were to say "Imagine this butterfly exactly as it is, but ugly instead of beautiful."

Ludwig Wittgenstein

My heart is like a flame turned upside down.

Guillaume Apollinaire

When his psychiatrist urged him to struggle with reality, he responded: "Doctor, I wrestled with reality for 40 years and I am happy to state that I finally won."

James Stewart in "Harvey"

Poetry, like the moon, does not advertise anything.

William Blissett

We are the words in 1920 silent movies.

Paul Carroll

Nobody realizes that some people expend tremendous energy merely to be normal.

Albert Camus

Later never exists.

Author Unknown

You are not afraid to die. Why are you afraid to live?

Joanna Sparks

And Satie . . . I can tell you something about him that will perhaps seem only amusing. But it is very significant. He had died, and we all went to his apartment, and under his blotter on his desk we all found our letters to him — unopened.

Jean Cocteau

It is easier to enter heaven than to pass through each other's eyes.

Saint Geraud

Life must go on. I forget just why.

Author Unknown

Yet some things you miss and some things you lose by keeping your arm outstretched.

Author Unknown

In Japan we have the phrase *Shoshin*, which means "beginners mind." The goal of practice is always to keep our beginner's mind. Our "original mind" includes everything within itself. It is always rich and sufficient within itself. This does not mean a closed mind, but actually an empty mind and a ready mind. If your mind is empty, it is always ready for anything; it is open to everything. In the beginner's mind there are many possibilities; in the expert's mind there are few.

Shunryu Suzuki

I'm looking for the face I had before the world was made.

W.B. Yeats

So much of adolescence is an ill-defined dying.

Theodore Roethke

And as we stray further from love we multiply the words. Had we remained together we could have become a silence.

Yehuda Amichai

Silver Departures

Now all my teachers are dead except silence.

W.S. Merwin

One in my hand, one in the air, and one in you.

Saint Geraud

In the spectrum there are no boundaries: each language can divide it into as many, or as few, sections as it chooses. When it was first realized that some of our shades of color were absent from the Homeric epics, it was suggested that Homer must have been colour blind.

Stephen Ullmann

Memory is incomplete experience.

J. Krishnamurti

To confront a person with his shadow is to show him his own light.

Carl Jung

Because nothing happens where definition is its own excuse for being, the map is as it was; a diagram of how the world might look could we maintain a lasting, perfect distance from what is.

Mark Strand

And I recall an account of Trollope going up to
London to pick up a rejected manuscript from a
publisher, getting on the train to return home,
laying the bulky bundle on his lap face down, and
beginning a new book on the back pages of the
rejected one.

Author Unknown

What if your knees bent the other way, what
would a chair look like?

Author Unknown

I have died so little today, friend, forgive me.

Thomas Lux

Perfection is a masculine desideratum, while
woman inclines by nature to completeness.

Carl Jung

A friend of mine took a Zen Buddhist monk to
hear the Boston Symphony perform Beethoven's
Fifth Symphony. His comment was "Not enough
silence!"

Winthrop Sargent

A language is a map of our failures.

Adrienne Rich

"Is it on?"

Three-year-old boy holding ball-point pen.

And he told about an interview he had once
with Barney Oldfield, the great racing driver. He
had asked Oldfield why he always seemed to be
involved in automobile accidents when driving in
street traffic. Oldfield replied that he was never
able to think clearly when traveling at less than a
hundred miles an hour.

It is the job of poetry to clean up our word-
clogged reality by creating silences around things.

Stephen Mallarme

Roots and wings. But let the wings grow roots
and the roots fly.

Juan Ramon Jimenez

Picasso insisted that everything was miraculous
— it was miraculous he said, that one did not melt
in one's bath.

It is not the failed relationships which influence
our life — they influence our death.

Anaïs Nin

Do you ever make silly mistakes? It's one of my very few creative activities.

Len Deighton

If all your bones were candles, your face would still be a dark answer.

Saint Geraud

On some hill of despair the bonfire you kindle can light the great sky — though it's true of course to make it burn you have to throw yourself in . . .

Galway Kinnell

Poetry is not an occupation, but a verdict.

Leonard Cohen

That which is one is one. That which is not one, is also one.

Chiang Tzu

Smoke. Remember who lets you go.

W.S. Merwin

*Silver
Departures*

Not dark, but on the contrary, charged with so much light it looks dark, because things are now packed so closely together. We see it with our teeth.

John Ashbery

Just because everything is different doesn't mean anything has changed.

Irene Poter

Do unto others as they wish, but with imagination.

Marcel Duchamp

The foot feels the foot when it feels the ground.

Buddha

Astronomer fears hostile attack: would keep life on earth a secret.

Newspaper headline

Neurophysiologists will not likely find what they are looking for outside their own consciousness, for that which they are looking for is that which is looking.

Keith Floyd

When I have to cut tapes, in the places where the speaker sometimes pauses for a moment — or sighs, or takes a breath, or there is absolute silence — I don't throw that away, I collect it. I splice it together and play back the tape when I'm at home in the evening.

Heinrich Böll

Truth has very few friends and those few are suicides.

Author Unknown

Kiss the flame and it is yours.

Thomas Lux

It doesn't matter if the water is cold or warm if you're going to have to wade through it anyway.

Teilhard de Chardin

That's how it goes, my friend. The problem is not falling captive, it's how to avoid surrender.

Nazim Hikmet

The basis of optimism is sheer terror.

Oscar Wilde

Silver
Departures

I believe there are more urgent and honorable
occupations than the incomparable waste of time
we call suffering.

                                                    Colette

You are always telling a dream. When do you
dream it?

                                            Antonio Porchia

Truth is a lie.

                                              Pablo Picasso

If you have any notion of where you are going,
you will never get anywhere.

                                                  Joan Miro

And what, after all, is the poem but the constant
threading of a needle? You have used the same
thread over and over, sewing clouds, sewing a
damaged heart, perfecting the things you know
well.

                                            Norman Rosten

The eskimos had fifty-two names for snow
because it was important to them: there ought to
be as many for love.

                                          Margaret Atwood

Everyone is indispensable.

Jean Renoir

But to say what you want to say, you must create another language and nourish it for years and years with what you have loved, with what you have lost, with what you will never find again.

George Seferis

My neighbor Howard says his mother saved everything. His mother made little cloth bags to hold pieces of string, each bag carefully labelled as to the length of the pieces. After her death they found one small bag of string labelled "too short to save."

Helen Bevington

All that is visible around us is in itself inexpressible, whereas what's expressible is within us, in itself, invisible.

Avigdor Arikha

The chief object of education is not to learn things but to unlearn things.

G.K. Chesterton

For example, everyone automatically assumes that the present is the result of the past. Turn it around, and consider whether the past may not be a result of the present. The past may be streaming back from the now, like the country as seen from an airplane.

Alan Watts

Coincidence, if traced far enough back, becomes inevitable.

Hineu

I have come one step away from everything. And here I stay, far from everything, one step away.

Antonio Porchia

We can't leave the haphazard to chance.

N.F. Simpson

Picasso often said that painting is a blind man's profession.

I do not know how to leap from the shore of today to the shore of tomorrow. The river carries, meanwhile, the reality of this evening to forlorn and hopeless seas.

Juan Ramon Jimenez

It is related that Sakyamuni once cried out in pity for a yogin by the river who had wasted twenty years of his human existence in learning how to walk on water, when the ferryman might have taken him across for a small coin.

I have worked for years just to have people say, "So that's all Matisse is."

Henri Matisse

It is completely unimportant. That is why it is so interesting.

Agatha Christie

I was not looking for my dreams to interpret my life, but rather for my life to interpret my dreams.

Susan Sontag

Once, when a G.I. was visiting Picasso during the liberation of France he said that he could not understand the artist's paintings. "Why do you paint a person looking from the side and from the front at the same time?" Picasso asked, "Do you have a girlfriend?" "Yes," replied the soldier. "Do you have a picture of her?" The soldier pulled from his wallet a photograph of the girl. Picasso looked at it in mock astonishment and asked, "Is she so small?"

"Amateur" used to mean "lover" before it came to mean one who pursues a discipline for pleasure.

The present is the only thing that has no end.

Erwin Schrodinger

I am not interested in grasping precisely a man I know. I am interested only in exaggerating him precisely.

Elias Canetti

To return what exists to pure possibility; to reduce what is seen to pure visibility; that is the deep, the hidden work.

Paul Valery

We are happy when for everything inside us there is a corresponding something outside us.

W.B. Yeats

When television came roaring in after the war (World War II) they did a little school survey asking children which they preferred and why — television or radio. And there was this 7-year-old boy who said he preferred radio "because the pictures were better."

Alistair Cooke

My business is Circumference.

Emily Dickinson

Read my lips, forget my name.

William Stafford

And you are left, to no one belonging wholly,
not so dark as a silent house, nor quite so surely
pledged unto eternity as that which grows and
climbs the night.

Rainer Maria Rilke

One has not understood until one has forgotten
it.

Suzuki Daisetz

Being on time when the rest of the world is
behind gives the impression of being ahead.

Jean Luc Godard

What we think is less than what we know; What
we know is less than what we love; What we love
is so much less than what there is: and to this
precise extent, we are much less than what we are.

R.D. Laing

You must travel at random, like the first Mayans.
You must risk getting lost in the thickets, but that
is the only way to make art.

Tezcatillipoca

Call it a dream. It does not change anything.

Ludwig Wittgenstein

I have a good friend, Rudolf Serkin, the pianist,
a very sensitive man. I was talking to him one day
backstage after a concert and I told him that I
thought he had played particularly sensitively that
day. I said, "You know, many pianists are brilliant,
they strike the keys so well, but somehow you are
different." "Ah," he said, "I don't think you should
ever strike a key, you should pull the keys with
your fingers."

Andrew Wyeth

When they tell you to grow up, they mean stop
growing.

Tom Robbins

The curious paradox is that when I accept
myself just as I am, then I can change.

Carl Rogers

You walk on carrying on your shoulders a glass
door to some house that's not been found.
There's no handle. You can't insure it. Can't put it
down.

W.S. Merwin

Everyone who believes what he sees is a mystic.

Author Unknown

There are so many little dyings that it doesn't
matter which of them is death.

Kenneth Patchen

You know, I've read your last story, and I ought
to have returned it weeks ago. It isn't right. It's
almost right. It almost works. But not quite. You
are too literary. You must not be literary. Suppress
all the literature and it will work.

Colette to Georges Simenon

Five years ago that would have been a happy
ending.

Author Unknown

Stop looking for what seems to be missing. You
have everything you need to start with — nothing.

Author Unknown

I perhaps owe having become a painter to flowers.

Claude Monet

The whole order of things is as outrageous as any miracle which could presume to violate it.

G.K. Chesterton

It is to the poet a thing of awe that his story is true.

Isak Dinesen

"The empty mirror," he said. "If you could really understand that, there would be nothing left here for you to look for."

Zen

Thinking: freeing birds, erasing images, burying lamps.

Pablo Neruda

Night and morning are making promises to each other which neither will be able to keep.

Richard Shelton

"I'm sure [my memory] only works one way,"
Alice remarked. "I can't remember things before
they happen." "It's a poor sort of memory that
only works backwards," the Queen remarked.

Lewis Carroll

I imagine that yes is the only living thing.

e.e. cummings

You can only know after you've been it . . . and
in order to be it you've got to give up knowing you
know. It's a fantastic paradox.

Ram Dass

My whole life is waiting for the questions to
which I have prepared answers.

Tom Stoppard

Reality is bad enough. Why should I tell the
truth?

Patrick Sky

The mystery of life is not a problem to be solved
but a reality to be experienced.

Aart van der Leeuw

Silver Departures

Poetry will rob me of my death.

René Char

Between living and dreaming is a third thing.
Guess it.

Author Unknown

May my silences become more accurate.

Theodore Roethke

Over and over a star became a tear. If no two
are alike then what are we doing with these
diagrams of loss?

Adrienne Rich

I used to have a book of dreams but now I have
a name of eyes.

Ilona Baburka (primary grade)

A garden I tend whose blossom never existed.

Pablo Neruda

A story should have a beginning, a middle, and
an end . . . but not necessarily in that order.

Jean Luc Godard

Now, in the exacting twilight, to choose, not
what we shall do or how we shall live but to
choose the life whose dreams will hurt least in the
nights to come.

Yehuda Amichai

The Indians long ago knew that music was
going on permanently and that hearing it was like
looking out a window at a landscape which didn't
stop when one turned away.

John Cage

Burn all the maps to your body.

Richard Brautigan

For such is our task: to impress this fragile and
transient earth so sufferingly, so passionately
upon our hearts that its essence shall rise up
again, invisible, in us. We are the bees of the
invisible. . . . The Elegies show us engaged in this
work, the work of the perpetual transformation of
beloved and tangible things into the invisible
vibration and excitability of our nature, which
introduces new "frequencies" into the fields of the
universe.

Rainer Maria Rilke

Silver Departures

The final belief is to believe in a fiction, which you know to be a fiction, there being nothing else. The exquisite truth is to know that it is a fiction and that you believe it willingly.

Wallace Stevens

One must use a brazen lie to convince people of a reality of a higher and deeper order.

Jean Cocteau

Sleep faster. We need the pillows.

Yiddish proverb

There might actually occur a case where we should say, "This man believes he is pretending."

Ludwig Wittgenstein

Perhaps our heart is made of the answer that is never given.

René Char

If only there were a perfect word I could give to you — a word like some artichoke that could sit on the table, dry, and become itself.

Sandra Hochman

An artist is a dreamer consenting to dream of the actual world.

George Santayana

Tolstoy and his brother, when they were boys, formed a club, initiation into which required that the candidate stand in a corner for half-an-hour and *not* think of a white bear.

I do not mind lying, but I hate inaccuracy.

Samuel Butler

Time is not a road — it is a room.

John Fowles

The essence of spirit, he thought to himself, was to choose the thing which did not better one's position, but made it more perilous. That was why the world he knew was poor, for it insisted morality and caution were identical.

D.H. Lawrence

With every blindfold you burn, things recede.

Richard Kehl

Silver Departures

And all the time it's your own story, even when you think — "It's all just made up, a trick. What is the author trying to do?" Reader, we are in such a story: all of this is trying to arrange a kind of prayer for you. Pray for me.

William Stafford

We are the echo of the future.

W.S. Merwin

And it is always the same confession, the same youth, the same pure eyes, the same ingenuous gesture of her arms about my neck, the same caress, the same revelation. But it is never the same woman. The cards have said that I would meet her in life, but without recognizing her.

Paul Eluard

Happiness is being able to speak the truth without hurting anyone.

Federico Fellini

Nothing gives more assurance than a mask.

Colette

I came to my grief too late. All the hospital beds are full of impersonators.

Richard Kehl

Good style is the record of powerful emotion reaching the surface of the page through fine conscious nets of restraint, caution, tact, elegance, taste, even inhibition — if the inhibition is not without honor.

Arthur Quiller-Couch

"You certainly have a lovely baby." "That's nothing. You should see his photograph."

Author Unknown

There is not enough of nothing in it.

John Cage

To the sea? To the sky? To the world? Who knows? The stars descend, as usual to the river, carried by the breezes . . . the nightingale meditates . . . sorrow grows more lovely, and high above sadness a smile bursts into bloom.

Juan Ramón Jimenez

Look for a long time at what pleases you, and longer still at what pains you . . .

Colette

Smoke is made of shadow juice.

Evan Greger, age 5

Silver Departures

"Nothing," said Moon. "I was trying to face one way or the other and I got confused and fell over. Let that be my epitaph."

Tom Stoppard

A poem is always married to someone.

René Char

In the poetry contest in China by which the Sixth Patriarch of Zen Buddhism was chosen, there were two poems. One said: "The mind is like a mirror. It collects dust. The problem is to remove the dust." The other and winning poem was actually a reply to the first. It said, "Where is the mirror and where is the dust?" Some centuries later in a Japanese monastery there was a monk who was always taking baths. A younger monk came up to him and said, "Why, if there is no dust, are you always taking baths?" The older monk replied, "Just a dip. No why."

by way of John Cage

Each song is love's stillness. Each star is time's stillness, a knot of time. Each sigh is the stillness of the shriek.

Federico Garcia Lorca

Actually, light dazzles me. I keep only enough of it in me to look at night, the whole night, all nights.

Paul Eluard

I have spread my dreams under your feet: tread softly because you tread on my dreams.

W.B. Yeats

When a man changes he'll sign letters unread and let his photos develop forever, he'll order shoes and not take them, and he'll forget his coat in the wardrobe of strangers.

Yehuda Amichai

Here I am trying to live, or rather, I am trying to teach the death within me how to live.

Jean Cocteau

If the author had said "Let us put on appropriate galoshes," there could, of course, have been no poem.

Author Unknown

It's time again. Tear up the violets and plant something more difficult to grow.

James Schuyler

Another way of approaching the thing is to consider it unnamed, unnameable.

Francis Ponge

We all have reasons for moving. I move to keep things whole.

Mark Strand

The fish trap exists because of the fish. Once you've gotten the fish you can forget the trap. The rabbit snare exists because of the rabbit. Once you've gotten the rabbit, you can forget the snare. Words exist because of meaning. Once you've gotten the meaning, you can forget the words. Where can I find a man who has forgotten words so I can talk with him?

Chuang Tzu

Wait: I have one foot already through the black mouth of the first nothing.

Juan Ramon Jimenez

A well-known physicist in Britain once told Wolfgang Kohler, "We often talk about the three B's, the Bus, the Bath, and the Bed. That is where the great discoveries are made in our science."

Julian Jaynes

It matters immensely. The slightest sound matters. The most momentary rhythm matters. You can do as you please, yet everything matters.

Wallace Stevens

The being we do not know is an infinite being; he may arrive, and turn our anguish and our burden to dawn in our arteries.

René Char

There is a saying that "paper is more patient than man"; it came back to me on one of my slightly melancholy days. . . . Yes, there is no doubt that paper is patient.

Anne Frank

The dream-work . . . does not think, calculate, or judge in any way at all; it restricts itself to giving things a new form.

Sigmund Freud

There's a kind of waiting you teach us — the art of not knowing.

William Stafford

Silver Departures

Were it possible for us to see further than our knowledge reaches, and yet a little way beyond the outworks of our divination, perhaps we would then endure our sorrows with greater confidence than our joys. For they are the moments when something new has entered us, something unknown; our feelings grow mute in shy perplexity, everything in us withdraws, a stillness comes, and the new, which no one knows, stands in the midst of it and is silent.

Rainer Maria Rilke

It gets late early here.

Yogi Berra

Perhaps my life is nothing but an image of this kind: perhaps I am doomed to retrace my steps under the illusion that I am exploring, doomed to try and learn what I should simply recognize, learning a mere fraction of what I have forgotten.

André Breton

Poetry is innocent, not wise. It does not learn from experience, because each poetic experience is unique.

Karl Shapiro

Truly nothing is to be expected but the unexpected!

Alice James

Won't you come into the garden? I would like my roses to see you.

Richard B. Sheridan

In dreams begin responsibilities.

W.B. Yeats

Don't solve the problem, just give it up.

Author Unknown

I am writing the memoirs of a man who has lost his memory.

Eugene Ionesco

Reality can destroy the dream, why shouldn't the dream destroy reality?

George Moore

My own habitual feeling is that the world is so extremely odd, and everything in it so surprising. Why *should* there be green grass and liquid water, and *why* have I got hands and feet.

Don John Chapman

Silver Departures

✓ When you get there, there isn't any there there.

Gertrude Stein

So many things fail to interest us, simply
because they don't find in us enough surfaces on
which to live, and what we have to do then is to
increase the number of planes in our mind, so
that a much larger number of themes can find a
place in it at the same time.

Ortega y Gasset

Be obscure clearly.

E.B. White

✓ A woman tries to comfort me. She puts her
hand under my shirt and writes the names of
flowers on my back.

Mark Strand

Give me the madman's sudden insight and the
child's spiritual dignity.

Theodore Roethke

I don't paint things. I only paint the difference
between things.

Henri Matisse

Dreams are not made to put us to sleep, but to awaken us.

Goemans

The Chinese say that poetry is the direction of your will. If that is not enough, you add a sigh. If that does not express what you mean completely, you chant or sing it. If that is not enough, you move your arms and legs too; you dance. That is poetry.

Art is more than life can bear.

Francis Celentano

Everything should be as simple as it is, but not simpler.

Albert Einstein

I do not ask of God that he should change anything in events themselves, but that he should change me in regard to things, so that I might have the power to create my own universe, to govern my dreams, instead of enduring them.

Nerval

This book was set in Korinna by Eucalyptus Productions, Inc.
of San Diego
Cover art was separated by Color Graphics of San Diego
Printed at the Green Tiger Press